I0134287

Learn How I Made a FORTUNE while In college

Real-life Student Strategy Guide

AUTHOR & LIFE COACH

SHAUNTAE M. JORDAN, MBA

"COACH J"

Learn How I Made a Fortune While in College
Real-life Student Strategy Guide:
Get Paid, Get Noticed, Now!

Copyright © 2011 *Coach J*
All rights reserved. No part of this publication may be reproduced, distributed, or transmitted in any form or by any means, including photocopying, recording, or other electronic or mechanical methods, without the prior written permission of the publisher, except in the case of brief quotations embodied in critical review and certain other noncommercial uses permitted by copyright law. For permission requests, write to the publisher, addressed "Attention: Permission Coordinator" at the address below:

Ground Rules Publishing
P.O Box 4411
Rock Hill, SC 29732
groundrules.publishing@gmail.com
www.smjspeaks.com

Ordering information:
Quantity sales. Special discounts are available on quantity purchases by corporations, associations and other. For details, contact the "Special Sales Department" at the Ground Rules Publishing address above. Individual sales. Ground Rules publications are available through most book stores. They can also be ordered directly from Ground Rules publications or directly from www.smjspeaks.com.

Library of Congress
ISBN-100983828709
ISBN-139780983828709

Design and produced by *James* | msjamesin@gmail.com
Cover design & cover photography *Blugraphics* | www.blugraphics.com
Copy editing by *Leah Henry*

Printed in the United States of America

CONTENTS

PART 2

PART 3

PART 4

LETTER FROM THE AUTHOR

Hey you,

To introduce myself I am Shauntae M. Jordan, my son calls me mommy, my husband calls me love and I would have you call me Coach J. I am an empowerment coach and speaker on yet another journey to share with you (student) about How I Made a Fortune While In College.

I enjoy sharing with parents, students, corporations, administrators and everyone else on the subject How I Made a Fortune While in College! It's my story of persistence, perseverance, resiliency, motivation, and drive that allowed me to gradu-

ate with less debt in fact $60,000 worth of schol-
arships, grants, work-study and a part-time job. I
know you are probably thinking $60,000, hurry
up and show me the money.

When I think of my college experience earning
$60,000 was a great accomplishment, but I gained
much more! My fortune consisted of my uncover-
ing passion, building my network (relationships),
developing leadership skills, discovering my
strengths, conquering my weaknesses, and explor-
ing unlimited possibilities. I want you to recognize
the key word here is earned, no one just handed
over $60,000 bucks and said go get it. It required
that I worked hard, positioned myself for success,
and made several commitments never to quit.

In this book, I share with you my life lessons,
tools to help you get noticed, stand out and become
lifelong leaders. It is important that you gain money
for college; it is also just as important that you know
how to create and earn a fortune when you leave. I

will share with you how to create your own opportunities, develop beneficial relationships, how to overcome rejection, and share with you my roadmap as a Cum Laude Graduate from Winston-Salem State University with a Bachelor of Science Degree in Business Administration and later a Summa Cum Laude Graduate of University of Phoenix with a Masters of Business Administration.

By the end of this book you will be ready to conquer your education and any dreams that you desire. You, your family, and friends will find this book a valuable resource for years to come. It will inspire you to become the driver of your own success™.

Before you move forward, I must be honest with you! There are three types of students; those who make things happen, those who watch things happen, and those who wondered what happened at all. When I was in high school, I had a tendency to watch things happen. I did not have a clue what

I wanted to do after graduation, nor did I know where I was going to get money from when I did graduate. Like I said I watched things happen; I was not prepared and didn't have the grades that would get me a great deal of scholarships.

Somewhere between watching things happen and my mother telling me what needed to happen, I shifted my mindset into high gear. That change of attitude followed me all the way to where I am today.

Remember, it is not just about the message within this book, it's more about the drive within you and the results you want for your life!

My question for you is what type of student are you?

Much Love and success,

Coach J

FOREWORD

THE TITLE OF THIS WORK MIGHT SUGGEST THAT
its purpose is to appeal to the self-indul-
gent, materialistic side of the reader.
Attention grabbing, yes; but it becomes
quickly apparent that Ms. Jordan has bigger
things in mind. The prospective reader is
encouraged to consider that this work is both
elegant and profound. Its elegance exists in
both its style and brevity, but what really
stands out is the underlying message.

A walk through any book store reveals
shelves full of motivational and self-help mate-

rials, which demonstrates that this genre is clearly of interest to us. Yet in this sea of materials aimed at inspiring, stimulating, and motivating us, few works are as practical, warm and down to earth as this, Ms. Jordan's first published work. In reading it, I couldn't help but think of the most famous of American speeches, Abraham Lincoln's *"Gettysburg Address,"* which has been studied in depth and received international acclaim. The context of Lincoln's most famous oration is what brings to mind a parallel with this work. At that dedication of a cemetery the President of the United States took his turn following a two hour speech by the country's then most famous orator, Edward Everett (President of Harvard University and former U.S. Secretary of State, Governor of Massachusetts, and member of both houses of congress). As Everett quickly conceded, Lincoln said more in 2 minutes than he had in 2 hours. Like Lincoln, Ms. Jordan says more in a few pages than many of the renowned experts of the day say in many volumes.

Her message is a universal truth that she openly shares in her desire to help others find their underlying passions and abilities. She speaks of making a fortune, but demonstrates the value of work, commitment and relationships. Coming through personal adversity she shows where her inspirations, courage and determination came from and how her readers can design their own destiny. Not only does she reveal secrets of success and the importance of a positive attitude, but she lays out a step by step plan. Ms. Jordan boldly shows how to take on pitfalls like failure and fear; she teaches how to use them and turn misfortune into an advantage. This work also contains a treasure trove of practical ideas, tools and affirmations that can be applied by persons seeking an education.

While written and focused toward young people of or approaching college age, it must be emphasized that this work contains those principles of success that cross generations, culture and gender. For this reason I recommend it to anyone interested in getting into the driver's seat to steer their lives to higher ground or wherever it is they wish to go.

- DR. MYRON BROWN

PREFACE

T HE DAY I OPENED MY ACCEPTANCE LETTER TO Winston-Salem State University (WSSU); my life changed without me realizing it.

I was "grown" now, and I was ready to move out of my mom's house to make my own decisions.

When I arrived at Winston-Salem State University (WSSU) I unpacked a ton of clothes, large of amounts of food, and a BIG grin! I could do this; college could not be that difficult.

As I looked out my dorm window the tail

lights of my mom's vehicle and her wallet left campus.

I remember thinking, "how hard could this be?"

Tears began to fall from my face!

I was already learning my first college lesson. Never get too big for your britches 101.

Coach J, 2011
www.smjspeaks.com

PART 1

THIS IS YOUR COURSE

ASSESS THE PAST

HERE'S MY STORY — LIKE TO READ IT? WELL, here it goes... I was raised in a single parent home by my mother. My great-grandparents had a large influence in my life by allowing my Mother and me to live with the two. Although my mother and father were not together; she allowed my father into my life every other weekend. I remember on each of these weekends crying the entire time to return home. I guess I could tell that my father had his own agenda. My father would tell me he loved me, but my heart did not feel the love he verbally expressed. I would tell my mom I did not want to go back. This non-supportive relationship progressed throughout my young adult life.

As long as I can remember my mother worked very diligently to provide for us. I rarely heard her complain if at all, and she always made a way out of no way. When I was seven my mother married my stepfather, and we moved to a small city three hours from my great-grandparents home. This had to be the most stressful, life-changing, and heart-breaking experience ever. The move took us away from the two people who I knew loved me unconditionally and would give me the world. Shortly after the marriage my mother, stepfather, and I welcomed my brother into our family. Eight years of my life I was the only child but I was expected to "happily" welcome these two new people into my life. During the two years that we were away from my great-grandparents, I remember living unhappy and rebellious. Then out of nowhere I experienced loss again when my mother's husband passed away, leaving my mother a single-parent a second time.

We experienced much uncertainty and sadness that my mother decided to pack us up and move back to Rock Hill, SC. At this point in my life, I was in the fifth grade. Although faced with loss I was beginning to experience happiness again. I have to give it to my mom - her ambition for life and willingness to overcome adversity is the fuel that runs through my body. There were numerous times in my mother's life when she could have broken down and given up, she stood strong. My mother worked day and night to put my brother through private school and she provided us with a beautiful home. I was quite a handful of trouble in middle school but her strength endured those teenage years.

YOUR ATTITUDE MATTERS

I attribute my mother's attitude and momentum for life as the foundation for many of my values. One value that I believe highly in is perseverance - to never give up. My mother never gave up when faced with the loss of her husband. In fact, she seemed even more determined to live her life to the fullest. She showed her strong spirit when she opened her own business in less than six months. I must admit this is definitely where I learned the importance of a "can-do" attitude. When faced with challenges, struggles, or fear my mother's attitude remained positive and upbeat. My mother trusted in God and allowed Him to be her GPS (which she says means that "God Provides Strength"). My mother did not sit down and provide a curriculum about perseverance, self-esteem, and self-love her actions spoke wonders into my life. She never used the excuse that she was a single-mother; instead she became the designer of her own destiny.

These values were instilled in me; therefore, I was destined for success. Gaining success is about your attitude. Of course your story is different from my story. Your story could be worse or it could be better, but our attitude is the guide to our outcome. You may say to yourself, "easier said than done." I do believe that in life we are given three choices – the right way, the wrong way, or no way at all. The answer lies within your soul. There are tools, support systems, and several sources that can get you moving forward to the right way, but just as my mother worked through her pain you must decide for yourself where you want your destiny to take you.

CREATE YOUR SUCCESS

When dealing with your past you have to acknowledge pains and fear to progress. Acknowledging your pain does not mean you need to wallow in it. I share the story of my childhood relationship with my father because I want you to know my life was nowhere close to perfect. My relationship with my father during my early stages in life was the most unsupportive and sent me on emotional tailspins at times. Young girls need encouragement, support, and security – it is so special and important when these are given from a Father. Healthy relationships with our parents and loved ones help build our foundation. I must say my foundation seemed rocky and incomplete. I wanted to have that family experience where both parents were in the home, but I did not. This reality scarred me for some portion of my life...but the scars did not last forever, eventually they began to fade.

Prior to attending college my mother had invested much of her money into her business and did not have additional funding for my college expenses. I remember getting ready to go off to school and needing money for textbooks. I asked my father for that book money. "Nobody told you to go to college, and you should have gone to a community college or stayed home," he said. His cold response stuck with me as a hurtful memory for a long time. You would think out of the $60,000 that I eventually managed to gather for college costs, my father's contribution could have at least been $500 for books.

I was disappointed, defeated, afraid, and most of all empty. I am not here to rag on my father, but I must set the tone for you on how I did not allow my circumstances to be my life influencers. In fact I used my circumstance as part of my determination to be different and not a statistic because my father was not in the home. At that point in my life I decided, I had to be **B.R.A.V.E.**, which meant I had to **b**elieve, **r**each for my goals, **a**ccept responsibility, **v**ow to grow, and **e**volve. These five (5) steps contributed to my decision to avoid allowing anyone else to be the "Driver of *MY* Success™."

DESIGN YOUR TOMORROW

I can certainly attest to the fact where you are today does not determine where you will be tomorrow. You may be feeling down or awful about past choices or experiences, but do not allow that to set the beat to your rhythm of success. Instead, by deciding today and forever that you *will design your tomorrow;* you can achieve anything you set your mind toward. You may be questioning at this point,

"*How* can I design my future, when I don't have control of today?" That is a great question, and here is your answer. You must begin by *executing* your plan and *envisioning* your future.

When forecasters predict the weather they are making a hypothetical guess based on trends or patterns of what the weather will be like. I can take a hypothetical guess that because you are reading this book about how to make 60 grand while in college, you will very likely graduate with less debt and with more positive qualities and skills. I can almost guarantee that you will also be able to develop patterns of looking toward the future. Even before things happen if you begin to speak life into its core existence it will come to you. Have you read the popular books <u>The Secret</u> or <u>The Keys to the Law of Attraction</u>? If so you may recall their emphasis on the importance of a person-conscious of decisions that he or she makes.

I have heard on many occasions students asking, "How am I supposed to get into college if my grades are horrible in high school?" Some of you may have even been told before that "you are not good enough." Maybe your parents are divorced, or it could be that no one has ever even spoken to you about college. What if you are the one with parents in Corporate America, who never seem to have enough time to help you find money? Whatever the case, if you begin right where you are at this moment and take some necessary steps you will begin to position yourself for a wealthier, happier, and more successful life. I am glad you have decided to use this book as a tool to get closer to your destiny.

OWN YOUR SUCCESS

One thing I can say is that in high school I did not begin to apply myself until my eleventh and twelfth grade years. The student I had been while in school did what I was told to do and *nothing* else. I was in college prep classes not even thinking of college. In high school I thought my future consisted of only dating my boyfriend, hanging out with friends, and staying up late. When asked by my Guidance Counselor, what I wanted to do when I graduate, I never had an answer. I seemed to be in some daydream as though life was just going to happen, and I would get whatever was given to me.

I thought high school was simply mandatory. My experience was full of suspensions, fighting, and being in the Principal Office. I was great at talking back and arguing. I earned B's and C's, and did not believe in doing anything extra. Not until the day I sat in the Principals Office and was told that the path I was leading would take: me no where. I cannot forget the words said to me that day. "No one is going to want to hire you let alone accept you in a University. Shauntae, this is your life, you have three more days of suspension, and if you continue down this road you will have nothing."

I was devastated and felt horrible but had no one to blame but myself. What I had been thinking all along was confirmed by my Principal. He told me that I would be "nothing" and "no one would want me." I heard those words in my head for days and weeks.

As I sat in the Guidance Counselors Office during lunch later that year, I heard students speaking of being accepted into college. I was behind and at some point during that hour I decided that I could no longer live in the moment. I had to act, and I had to act fast. It was though a light bulb turned on and I realized that if I were going to *be* or *do* anything I could no longer be just the *passenger* of my life...I would need to sit in the driver's seat. I started taking my education and my life more seriously.

A couple of days later I began working in the Career Center of my high school. I would see all types of students come in and out. Many were preparing themselves for college and summer internships. While working in the Career Center, I began to think about my future more. What was I going to do after I left those hallowed halls of high school? Where was I going to go?

I began to reposition my life. I first became more active in high school. For example, I joined the Junior Achievement Team and increased my volunteer service. I started listening to what other students were doing to prepare themselves for their future. I asked how I could receive summer internships too. In fact, I began just applying for anything I could get my hands on. I was determined more than ever to become someone.

After writing my first resume, I believed I was on top of the world. This "take charge" attitude was what I needed to get me my first internship at First Union Bank. By working in the Career Center I had full access to Career and Guidance Counselors, who prepared me with mock interviews. I was so driven that I decided I would not only try to take on an internship and attend a Summer Enrichment Program at the College of Charleston but also I would also apply for Summer School at York Technical College to receive nine hours of free college credit during my eleventh grade year. The York Technical College opportunity was very competitive. I was one of 12 students out of the entire county of York to be selected. Who cared if *one* person believed I would not become anything? *I* was one person who began believing in *me*. I applied and with help from my Career Counselors (and the large amount of volunteer hours I earned), I was chosen. The experience was not the easiest, either. I was a high school student taking college classes. Classes were held all day, and no one motivated me to do my homework. In fact, no one prepared me for the experience. It required dedication, self-motivation, courage, determination, self-discipline, and perseverance. I wanted so badly to accomplish something in my life. I wanted to *learn* more, *experience* more, and *do* more with my time and life. To be honest and frank with you, I could no longer depend on anyone else, my success depended on *me*.

There are seven steps or "must-do" that I want to provide to help you achieve the best results.

Step 1:   You must *want* to achieve greater results in your life.

Step 2:   You must *agree* that your cir-

cumstance does not deter-
mine your future.

Step 3:   You must be willing to *change* habits or actions that are not developing you into a better person.

Step 4:   You must be *ready* to work hard.

Step 5:   You must *take* action.

Step 6:   You must remember that success starts with *you*.

Step 7:   You must do *whatever* it takes.

My question is: Are you ready to grab your destiny? If your answer is "yes," I am very excited! Begin to make it happen, now.

FEAR + BARRIERS = ACTION

Many people are scared of small insects like bees, ants, bugs, snake, etc. If they see any of these insects you will find them hiding or running away from the tiny creature. I am often amazed at how these folks become terrified even though they are twenty-times bigger than the insect. You may be one of them. Here you are, a 150-pound person frozen stiff with fear at the thought of a bug attack. As the insect comes closer, you can stand still and allow it to bite you, you can move out of its line of fire, or *you* can attack. Whichever you choose, you at that moment are forced to make a decision. You have to *do* something. That something is called ACTION!

When faced with fear of the unknown, we cannot just stand there and allow life to take us by the hand. You need to be prepared and make a decision about what you want to achieve and just do it. Fear can handicap you to the point where you think that life is not worth living. We often hide behind the

shadow of our fears or run away from challenges because we are afraid to fail. Fear
must be acknowledged. The first step in rec-
ognizing fear is being honest with yourself
about the fear you are facing. There were
numerous fears I faced in college. I feared I
was not smart enough to get through college.
I thought that I would not make friends, and
I would be lonely. One of my greatest fears
was the Cashiers Office at Winston-Salem
State University, not acquiring enough money
to complete my education.

ACKNOWLEDGE FEAR

I was so scared to knock on the Dean's door.
Maybe it was because the secretary that sat
at the front desk glared at me each time I
passed the office. Her glasses hung slightly
toward the tip of her nose; she would look
over her glasses and without words you knew

she did not want you to ask her any questions. I was afraid to enter her office with great expectations that she would turn me around, but I had no choice because I had less than a week to get myself some money for college. So when you have your back against the wall fear forces you to take action.

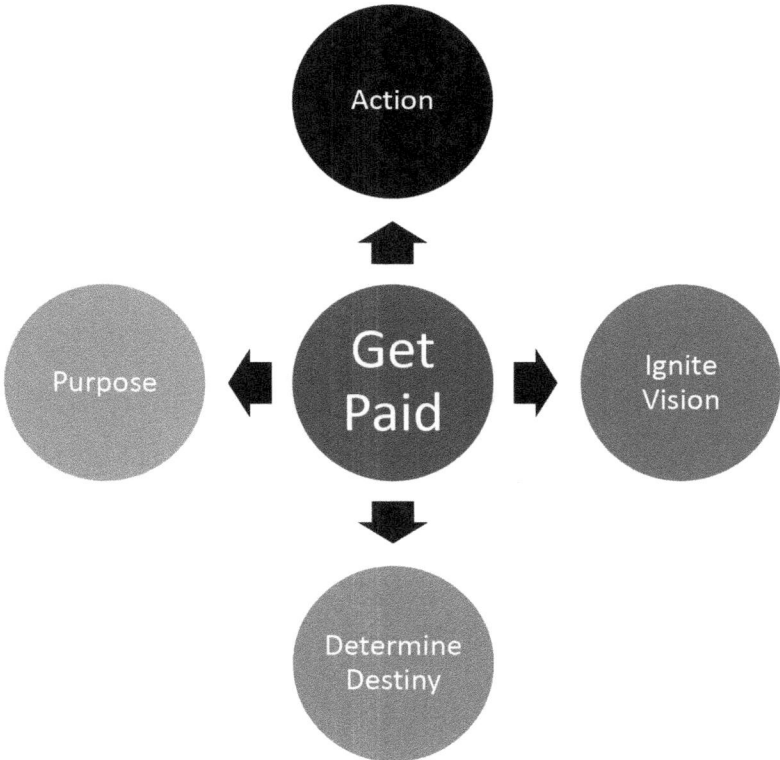

Action

Purpose

Get Paid

Ignite Vision

Determine Destiny

After class one-day I approached the office and requested to speak with the Dean of Business Administration. Of course the Secretary's response was that he was busy and I would have to schedule a better time to speak with him. I began frantically explaining my "emergency," and how it was very important that I met with Dr. King as soon as humanly possible. My sob story did not make the situation better. She was not trying to hear all of that. So I followed the rules and scheduled an appointment.

The day came to meet with Dr. King. When I walked into his office, I felt so intimidated. There were books wrapped around his office from floor to ceiling. *What was I doing in here,* I asked myself. I had no experience speaking with Deans or anyone else who had the responsibility of keeping an office for that matter. As I sat on the couch my heart was pounding. I had not a clue of what to say.

All I knew was that I better get myself some money or I was trekking it back to South Carolina.

Dr. King was not the kind of man who wore a big smile. My first thought was that he was going to cut me down and throw me to the wolves. I went for it anyway – full speed ahead. "Hello, I am Shauntae Barnette, from Rock Hill, SC, and I am a freshman here. I am majoring in Business Administration. I need some money for college or I am going back home." This was followed by a long pause… I kept going. "See, I am a good student. I am paying out-of-state tuition, and I have an outstanding bill at the Cashiers Office waiting for me to pay it. My mom doesn't have any money and I don't want to go home. So the question is do *you* have any money for me so I can stay in school?"

As I share this story with you, I am laughing. I do not even know if I were breathing when those words began to erupt from my mouth. Many of my friends would probably already know that I had a handful of tissues, and I was crying by this time. My glasses were foggy making it hard to see. Dr. King, a distinguished well educated leader, stood over me looking somewhat surprised and humored.

1. DETERMINE DESTINY

At this point I have acknowledged that I was afraid of not being successful in college. My greatest fear is that I would have to return home because of lack of money. This was not an option - I had to evaluate my decisions. Yes, that is right *you* must evaluate your decisions.

Dr. King popped two big questions. "Shauntae, you came to college without any money? Couldn't you have gone to a college in South Carolina?" I was shocked! I thought he *wanted* students to come to Winston-Salem State University. He doubted my decisions, and it forced me to evaluate my choices. Why had I chosen *this* particular college? There are plenty of great schools in South Carolina. Why had I not planned better? I was losing ground in this meeting and losing ground fast. I looked Dr. King in the face and I said, "I selected Winston-Salem College because it is the place that I want to obtain my education. The technology is great, and…I got accepted." What a lame answer some would say, but it was *my* answer. Dr. King gave me some thoughtful, profound response, and I sat there emotionally defeated. It looked as I was *not* going to have the money I needed by the end of the week.

2. FINDING YOUR PURPOSE

When I arrived back to my dorm room I must admit, I felt like a failure. Although Dr. King advised that he would assist me I thought that I had not done enough to prepare for my future. I had to articulate my purpose. *Why* did I select WSSU? I had been introduced to this Campus by a program known as Campus Connections. This program afforded me the opportunity to visit different historical black colleges and universities. I remembered the day we entered WSSU's beautiful campus and the warm smile that greeted me. We walked into Thompson Building, which would later become my second home and gold mine. The student government, school administrators, and a remote control that changed the appearance of a conference room were my deciding factors, I was sold - this was the school.

Define Your Purpose

Why are *you* going to college? What college have you selected and why? Have your parents been telling you that you need to attend a certain college all your life? Maybe your friends from high school all have decided to attend the same college? Do you have a boyfriend/girlfriend who will be attending a particular University? Do you like the way the campus looks? These are important questions when articulating your purpose.

When you articulate your purpose you are defining your reason for existence. I remember sitting in my dorm slinging tears and a little snot. I called my mother explaining that I did not have enough money, and I did not know what to do. As I sat there I began to recall the reasons, I wanted a higher education. What was it that I wanted to do or achieve while being there? What impact could I make in the four years of being a student at Winston-Salem State University?

I wanted to gain new experiences, learn from those experiences, and take my knowledge back home and teach others. No way was I going to leave Winston-Salem State. I had invested my time and my money. Most of all, I wanted to make a difference in my family. I desired to set the tone for generations to come. Quitting was not allowed.

I began to start speaking positive things to myself. I took notes from that tough little character named Thomas the Caboose. I kept telling myself I think I can, I think I can. I know I can! That attitude and the knowledge of my purpose set the tone for the next four years of my college experience.

3. TAKE ACTION

What I have failed to tell you is that I was seeking someone else to fix *my* problem. Dr. King was right I did have other options of attending colleges in South Carolina. However, I would be in the same position at one of those Schools asking where to get tuition money. I was not a terrible academic student in high school; however, I was not at the top of my graduating class, either. Upon leaving high school my intentions were very clear, I wanted to have independence, I wanted to do what I thought was right by attending college, and I wanted to get what many of people believe they deserve. Dr. King's motive was not to discourage me from attending WSSU but was instead to realize that I had to make intentional decisions for my life. I needed to know what I wanted and capitalize on reasons for doing what I do. Therefore, it was necessary to have a plan and not expect others to *give* me what I thought I deserved.

4. IGNITE A VISION

A vision describes where you see yourself within the next couple days, months, or years. It can be so much more than that, however.

Your vision statement is your inspiration, the framework for all your dreams, goals, and experiences. A vision is your WHY reminder. *Why* do you exist? *Why* are you are going to college? *Why*? What makes a vision statement unique is that it is for you. An important reminder is to allow your vision to be big, use your imagination, and dare to dream. A vision statement captures your passion, your reason for being!

My College Vision: I want to become a business owner. I have selected Business as my major. Part of my plan is to work for a fun, creative company that will allow me to gain experience in Business Management and Operation.

The one thing you will discover in creating your vision is that it is your vision and everyone does not see your vision the way that you do. Your goals, dreams, or plans do not exist until *you* believe and work at them wholeheartedly. If you do not believe in your vision it will be very easy for someone to distract you from your destiny. It is important that you write your vision down and place it in front of you daily.

After writing my vision I used it in my daily activities while in school. Every time I spoke with the Dean or other students they began to know what I wanted to do in my life. I began to speak my vision often, the Dean felt compelled to become involved in it. You know your vision possesses power when others begin to work on your behalf to see the vision come alive.

The Dean of the Business Department selected me to be a Student Ambassador for a Corporate Partner. I was also elected as the president of the Business Club. If that was not enough, I was awarded over $25,000 in scholarships over the next three and a half years of my college experience because of essays

I wrote and my participation in extracurricular activities.

Take a moment to write *your* vision:

_____

_____

_____

_____

_____

_____

_____

_____

_____

_____

_____

_____

_____

_____

_____

_____.

PART 2

DRIVING 101

HEADING IN THE RIGHT DIRECTION

WHILE DRIVING IT IS ALWAYS IMPOR-tant that you look ahead. Do not look to the side or make a habit of look-ing down. Have you ever been in a traffic jam before? All you see are red brake lights, car after car for miles. If for one moment you take your eye off the road while driving in this kind of traffic you will more than likely hit the car in front of you. Not looking ahead makes you less prepared to stop, and you are often caught off guard and unable to make lane changes if necessary.

Looking ahead as this relates to your life is just as important as looking to make sure that you do not hit the car in front of you. Even before you fill out your college applications you must be able to look forward to your goals. For example, if you are interested in getting a job it is important to have the necessary experience and certain credentials to be considered. By looking ahead you can prepare, which helps you make wiser choices and decisions. It requires planning. Most of us do not enjoy spending the time it takes to plan. However, the investment you make in planning will bring you such a large reward. Being prepared will help you to stay calm whenever obstacles or roadblocks get in your way.

SLOW DOWN

When driving through neighborhoods or parking lots you have to go speeds some-times of five miles per hour or less. I am cer-tain the reason that so many parking lots and neighborhoods have speed bumps is that someone endangered themself or others by trying to go 40 miles per hour in five miles per hour driving zone. The speed bumps were placed in these areas because of someone's lack of making the right decision to slow down. I am sure you have had some road-blocks placed in your life before. You more than likely did not realize that these blocks were placed there as a means of making sure you slow down before making hasty decisions.

As an Instructor, I see firsthand how stu-dents adopt stress as a life-style. Students are constantly complaining about their lack of time and how frustrated they are with their classes. I have students who work full-time jobs, have a full class load, and wonder why they do not have the energy or time to complete their assignments. Do not get me wrong, just because someone has a great deal of responsibilities does not mean he or she will not be able to juggle a heavy schedule. While in college I had a part-time job at Target, a work-study commitment, a full class load of 12 credits, and a large involvement in extracurricular activities. So you see I know exactly what it is like to be stretched thinly. I could not apply 100% of my time into any one thing. It is a wonder that I graduated Cum Laude with a 3.43 GPA Hallelujah! I wish someone told me what I am about to tell you...Slowwwwwww down!

I was constantly making mistakes and had many "do over's" because I was doing too much and not managing my time. Therefore, when I see students flustered because of lack of sleep and inadequate planning I simply want to holdup a yield sign or place a speed bump in front of them so they can change their pace. The high speed of life has us all wanting to get to the finish line even without us finishing and accomplishing our goals with the greatest results.

You cannot enjoy the sun after it has set! Begin to enjoy every moment of your high school or college experience. It is important to plan, to set goals, to make great grades, but it is equally important to maximize every moment. Take time to slow down, to explore your campus and the world it has to offer. Try your best to never overextend yourself, and this will afford you more time and ability to focus on what is currently at hand.

Every year it never fails, my classrooms are full with bright students. They are so excited to begin the semester and have great intentions on completing the course. By mid-semester I can count the students on two hands that will be in my class that day. Mid-semester the full class has become much smaller and the remaining students are unmotivated and exhausted. Finally, the end of the semester brings less than half my original set of students to class, and those remaining are barely able to commit to another day. They at one time had a high expectancy to succeed, but experience burnout very quickly after mak-ing irrational decisions during the semester; that now have them scattering around to find extra credit to fulfill their less than satisfactory grades. Do not let this be you!

POSITION YOURSELF FOR SUCCESS

I remember when I first took Driver's Educa-tion. My driver's education teacher was a stickler for making sure that we positioned the driver's seat to best accommodate each individual. If I got in the driver's seat after someone tall had been driving I would have strain to reach the gas pedal. The mirrors were in awkward positions,to be comfortable and safe I had to make adjustments. It required that even before I turned on the ignition that my seat was properly positioned.

To be successful you must position yourself before you set forth on your journey to achieve your goals. Imagine yourself stepping into the BIG world of college and not being prepared. An important reminder to you is that success does not come to you because of your background, your relatives, your talents, or your great looks. Success comes from positioning yourself to be ready to make a move when the opportunity presents itself.

One thing I have learned is that you cannot determine where you are going if you do not know *who* you are or *what* your current position is. You will not get the results you desire without knowing those important factors. I have never been one to give good directions nor have been a great student of receiving directions from others. Whenever I am lost and I seek guidance, the person I am speaking to always asks, "Where are you located or what landmark is around you?" When I tell them I donot know, they usually reply with, "Well, I cannot help you if you do not know where you are located."

If you recall I told you I went to the Deans office asking for scholarship money. He asked me what my goals were and why I had chosen Winston-Salem State University. I did not have a clear answer for him. Where was I, and where did I want to end? If I knew what I know now, I would have chosen to use the seven steps listed on the next page to position myself to win.

TIPS FOR SUCCESS POSITIONING

1.   **Be patient.** Realize that positioning yourself for success does not happen overnight. It takes time but you have to start getting the plan in motion.

2.   **Equip yourself with the right tools.** Make sure you have the necessary education and qualifications.

3.   **Network.** Check your cell phones Contacts, your Facebook Friends, Twitter Pages, past Teachers, and your Friend's Parents for resources.

4.   **Get involved.** Participate in school activities and community activities. Be aware and be "in the know."

5.   **Be proactive.** Do not just wait for things to happen.

6.   **Create your own opportunity and be ready when the opportunity comes.** If you want to get a job, gain money for college or get a promotion, be ready to open the door of opportunity before it knocks.

7.   **Make the decision *"to want"* to succeed.** Decide that you want to succeed!

DO NOT LOSE CONTROL OF THE WHEEL

Have you ever lost control of the steering wheel? When this happens most people try to over-correct, making the situation worse. In snow and ice storms we are told to allow the vehicle to go in the direction the ice is taking the car. Never try to jerk your steering wheel in the opposite direction because you will lose control of the car. You have big dreams and aspirations. You can plan for your life to go one way, but it certainly does not always go the way you plan. For months or years you have envisioned going to your number-one pick college, but discover that you are not accepted. What do you do? Sometimes dreams and plans can be deferred. It causes your life to shift and go in another direction. You may have to change the course and move in the direction that life is leading you. When we lose control we are faced with STRESS! This in return can create health problems, mental strain, fear, and major setback.

If you are a highly driven person you most likely do not like the idea of losing your grip on a situation. Often you can experience anxiety created by not being in control. There are techniques available that can help you avoid panic.

MANUEVER PASS STRESS

First, find something you *can* control, like yourself. You have the right to control *how* you will react to situations. You can control your attitude! When circumstances appear to have no hope, it is important that you maintain a positive attitude.

Second, learn how to be an influencer of your reactions. When you react with a negative attitude it seems as though the problem lasts forever. If by chance you begin to think positive about the situation and find the silver lining the solution seems to reach you even faster.

Third, check your attitude and make sure you are not making the situation worse.

KEEP A CLEAR VISION

When selecting a college you have many choices and just as many majors within that college to choose from. I challenge you to begin thinking about which college would be just right for you. I encourage you to select a major based on *your* dreams and hopes and not that of your parents or friends. So often students are tempted to make school selections based on where their best friend will be attending or his or her parents have been suggesting forever. When you make decisions about your life based on the visions that others have for you, you will begin to lose focus of *your* dreams and take on the hopes others have for you.

I was told that Business Management was too broad a major and that I should select Accounting or Computer Science instead. Because I knew what I wanted to accomplish in my college experience, I did not allow other's visions to interrupt my vision for myself. The only time your vision should change is if *you* change the vision. This means if you decide

the college of your choice or major is not working toward your vision it can be changed to
allow you to get closer to the goal or dream
you have for yourself. I believe it is important to
listen to loved one's experiences and accept
constructive criticism, but make sure you are
prepared to discuss *your* dreams with them.
Once you take a lead on your life, others will
take you seriously and know that you have a
plan. Your family, teachers, and friends want
the best for you. Therefore, be ready to share
your vision at all times.

PART 3

PUTTING IT IN MOTION

START YOUR ENGINE: INITIATE NEW RELATIONSHIPS

NETWORKING IS ONE OF THE MOST VALU-able tools you will use in your life-time. I wrote the word "lifetime" because networking will be a part of your life forever. Many of you have participated in some form of networking without even realiz-ing what you were doing. Have you ever played in sports or been a member of a Club or Organization? Do you have friends with parents? Of course you do! Therefore, every time you meet someone at an event or spend time with your friends, it is an opportunity to network. Networking is about gaining knowledge, learning about yourself and how the world operates.

The key to obtaining any goal, career, or opportunity is that you must network and develop new relationships. I managed to meet every administrator on campus. That was one of my **key elements** in making 60k while in college. I knew no stranger. I made it known what I needed, who I was, and what I wanted to accomplish. I also made great friends while in college. These persons were positive, provided constructive feedback, provided honesty, and wanted to see me succeed – **these relationships are priceless!** If you do not have any friends like that or if your friends are negative, they are not your friends and you need to initiate new relationships.

ROAD TRIP: PLAN FOR SUCCESS, PREPARE FOR FAILURE

Have you ever heard that success falls on the lap of those who *wait*? I am certain if you ask any successful individual *how they obtained success,* the answer will not state success fell out of the sky. Instead they would tell you that they experienced failure after failure before they achieved success. When asked the question what does failure mean to me? I find myself telling people that my failures have become my footstool to obtaining success. I use each failure to get closer to my destiny by not allowing it to stop my progress. Nothing frustrates me more than when failures seem to be in the lead. However, to elevate, you must prepare for failure. I know you are probably thinking I am making a mistake by writing that, but it is true. Your ultimate goal is to obtain success.

So claim your successes and be ready for failure.

RE-START YOUR ENGINE: BE PERSISTENT AND ADOPT PERSEVERANCE

If no one has ever told you **NO** before, thank you for the honor to tell you first. **NO!** Many salespersons state that for every ten "no's" there is a "yes." I cannot tell you how many scholarship applications I filled out! I *can* say that I was beginning to run out of words to write. Every day I checked the mailbox for a response to my applications and every day I would at least receive one response of, "Thank you for applying for this scholarship, but we have made our selection and we have decided to award this scholarship to a student who meets the requirements more closely."

The Business Department money train finally came to a close; I exhausted the funds that were available to me. Still determined to find additional monies to continue my college education, I began seeking funds from other departments. I remember even seeking money from the Biology Department. I was certain that if it were money out there it needed to be in my hand.

This is the same attitude you must adopt. You should continue asking until you find a "**YES.**"Remember if someone tells you "no" once it does not mean they will tell you "no" again. I worked in the Financial Aid Department on my college campus. I would hear fist hand what new scholarships were available. I remember asking every semester for book vouchers. I inquired about book vouchers almost every day; the financial aid representative prepared a check for me the beginning of each semester! **Persistence pays off: Can**

you say "cha-ching?" The $600 Book Vouchers per semester equaled to a total of $4800 towards book purchases throughout my college experience.

SHIFT YOUR GEARS FOR SUCCESS

Just **A.S.K. (A**rticulate, **S**hare,gain and use **K**nowledge**)**

Have you asked for what you want? Do you *know* what you want? Do you know how to get what you need? You must ask. The hardest thing for some is simply asking for what they want. The question is,"How do I ask someone for money, Coach J?" There are three steps in **ASK**ing.

The first step is to **articulate** your goals. What is it that you want? Where do you see yourself? Goals should be very **SMART (S**avvy, **M**easurable, **A**ttainable, provide **R**esults, follow a

Target date). Goals should be very clear and specific, so well written others do not have to ask repeatedly what you are stating. Goals should also be measurable; for example you need $45,000 to attend schools for four years. Your goal statement must have numbers included to know exactly what is necessary to determine the progress. The goal should also be achievable. There is no need to write an unattainable goal that want be achieved. The goals need to create results and have a timeline for the goal's achievement.

The second step in **ASK**ing is **sharing**. You need to recognize those individuals who will add value to your goals and share your vision with them. This in return allows others to know and understand your need, your dream, and your plan. Sharing your goals hold you accountable. I remember sharing the goal with Dr. King that I wanted to meet new people over the next couple of months. He nominated me to participate in the Chancellor's Leadership Conference.

The final step in **ASK**ing provides you the opportunity to gain **knowledge**. The persons who you are asking for money may not have the financial resources, but they might possess the knowledge on how to obtain additional resources. On numerous occasions I would speak to people around my campus about scholarships or internships. The majority of the people I spoke to directed me in the direction of finding money. ASKing allows you to save time. The more knowledgeable you become on the matters of gathering finances for education, the more likely you will be to receive funding. Allow yourself to ask for what you want and I am certain you will gain financial resources and knowledge that you did not know was available.

YOUR TRIPLE A (AAA)

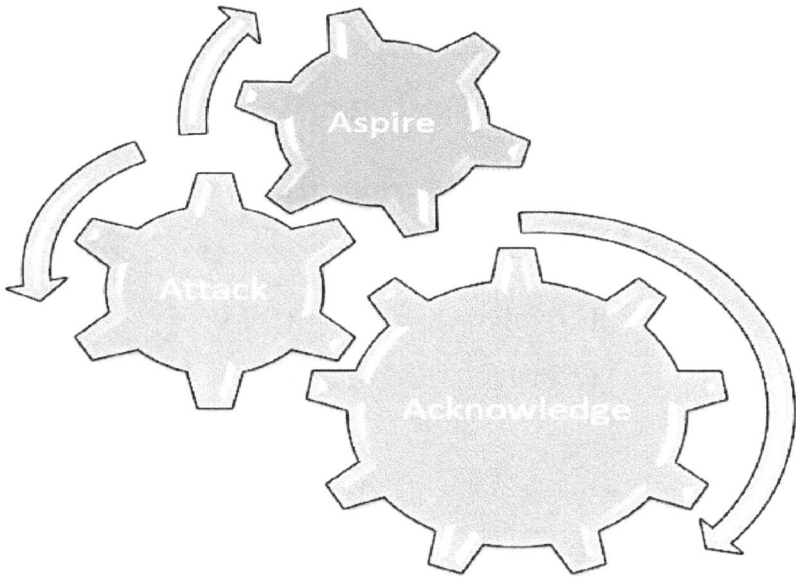

Here is an example for clarity: Your success would be to pass your classes. State the grade you want to earn, what it will take to earn it and what difference will it make in your education.

1. **Acknowledge** (read the following examples and fill in the blanks).

a.   I acknowledge that my course load is too heavy (15 credits or more) or too stressful (3 or more challenging classes in one semester).

b.   I acknowledge that I may not have enough study time because of my over commitment to other things.

c.   _____

_____

_____

2.   **Attack**

a.   I will attack my class work assignments directly after class instead of waiting to the last minute to study.

b.   _____

_____

_____

_____

c.   _____

_____

_____

_____

3.   Aspire

    a.   I am determined to pass
my class with grades no less
than a B.

    b.   _____

_____

_____

_____

    c.   _____

_____

_____

_____.

PART 4

MAPPED FOR SUCCESS

---

11 KEY STEPS TO DEVELOPING YOUR MAP TO SUCCESS

1. Get Drive

2. Believe In Yourself.

3. Have Ambition.

4. Deliver with Determination.

5. Take Action.

6. Define Your Strengths (What are you

good at doing: speaking, making
friends, helping others, etc.?).

7.   Make Intentional Decisions
     (Be mindful of every choice you
     make).

8.   Know that Quitting is not an Option.

9.   Develop Positive Relationships.

10. Gain Confidence (know who you
     are, discover what brings you joy).

11. Define What You Want and Seek
     Results.

THE "CHECK"POINTS
Shauntae's Financial Aid Transcript

Tuition - 1998-2002 est.	Fees (Full-time Student) 12 & Above credit hours	Total Expenses per Semester
Tuition Required Fees	4,510	4,510
Health	63.50	63.50
Student Activities	108.00	108.00
Athletic	187.50	187.50
Campus Center	78.00	78.00
Education & Technology	95.00	95.00
Assoc. of Student Government	10.00	10.00
Transportation	10.00	10.00
Health Insurance	263.00	263.00
Total		**$5325**

Room	2030.00
Meals	587.80
Total	**$2617.80**

Expenses Per Semester		
Total Tuition & Fees	$5325	
Room & Meals	$2617	
Books	$600	
Total Per Semester	**$8542 x 2**	**$17, 084 Tuition per year**

Total Tuition Cost (Out- of –State Tuition 4-years) $68,336

Financial Source		Amount
Pell Grant	$3500 x 4 years	$14000
Work Study	$3000 x 4 years	$9000
WSSU Business Department Scholarship	$3125 x 4 years	$15000
WSSU Book Voucher	$1200 x 4 years	$4800
Private Scholarships	$500 x 4 years	$2000
Total Scholarships/ Grants		$44,800
*** Citi Financial Loan Payback		($16,600)

York Technical College Transfer Class 12 hr. credit	$8542	$8542 (Subtract from tuition)
Target- Part-time Job	$813 x 9 months	$7317
Total		**$15859**
Grand Total		**$60659**

THE JOURNEY

Visualize your results

a.   What is your ultimate goal?

_____

_____

_____

_____

_____

_____

_____

_____

_____

_____

_____

_____

_____

b.   What does your finish line look like?

_____

_____

_____

_____

_____

_____

_____

_____

_____

_____

_____

IDENTIFY YOUR NEED & DETERMINE YOUR FUTURE

1. What results do you want to achieve?

    _____

    _____

    _____

    _____

    _____

    _____

    _____

    _____

    _____

    _____

    _____

2. Where do you see yourself in 6 months to 5 years from now?

    _____

    _____

_____

_____

_____

_____

_____

_____

_____

_____

3.   What resources do you need to
     accomplish your outcome?

_____

_____

_____

_____

_____

_____

_____

_____

_____

_____

_____

4.   Who can help you achieve those
     results?

_____

_____

_____

_____

_____

_____

_____

_____

_____

_____

_____

_____

_____

_____

FINAL THOUGHTS...

In life there will be situations that question if all your efforts are worth it. You may find yourself asking is this really worth it? Can I really achieve the goals I set out to achieve? If I quit will that allow me to get something more rapidly? Those are just a few common questions that most leaders ask themselves. You are special it is very important that you stay focused and do not allow your wheel to spin out of control.

PART 5

USE YOUR TOOLS

SELF-PROMOTION IS KEY

Statement: "I'm only a student. I don't need a resume, and I don't have anything to list on a resume."

Answer: False.

- A Resume' is a passport to unlimited opportunities. It does not only summarize experiences, it is a work in progress that lists goals and accomplishments as they develop. There is no better time than your senior year of high school to begin writing your Resume' that will be re-written several times before and after you receive your college degree.

Let's bust some Resume' Myths:

Myth #1: "I am a student - I don't have any experience to list on my resume"

- If you are a high school student, think about clubs/organizations, course-work, or part-time jobs that you are a part of. Use your high school events as stepping stones for your college ac-complishments. When you become a freshman in college, drop the high school experience to recognize the fresh college accomplishments.

Myth #2: "I am not applying for a full-time job why do I need a Resume'?"

- Most people only seriously think about

their Resume' when they are apply-ing for a full-time job. As a high school or college Student, you may not be considering a full-time job search for a few years from now. You may also find that many part-time jobs do not expect college students to even have a Resume'. Because you are the driver of your own success you will now be a step above the fellow college student and job applicant who did not submit a resume. You will look very profes-sional and will more than likely receive the opportunity because you took an extra step.

Myth #3: "I am not applying for any jobs right now; I do not need a resume."

■ Practice makes perfect! There are only a few things worse than graduat-ing from College and not being prepared for an opportunity. Remember all the volunteer work you are doing needs to be placed on your Resume'. This will help you be more prepared and less stressed when you *do* apply for a job. The more you write a Resume' better you become.

Your Resume' should include the following items:

Demographic Information – to include your Name, your Contact Information (such as your residence, phone number, and e-mail address.); if your personal email account has a "nickname" within the address, consider opening another account solely for Employment and Business matters (in other words, shauntae.jordan@gmail.com is professional although sweetshauntae@gmail.com is not)

Education – start with the most recent degree you are working on and work your way backward; you can list your GPA if it is 3.0 or higher

Employment – list your current most recent job, followed by past positions you have held (most first-year students will have few jobs to list and that is okay)

Activities – What activities are you involved in on Campus? What Clubs and Organizations did you participate in during High School? Write them down.

Volunteer Experiences – if you volunteered for any organizations or participated in any charitable events in high school, speaks of your experiences; Community Outreach is highly favored in the world of employment.

Coursework – What classes are you taking this semester? Did you take Advanced Placement classes in High School? You do not need to list every class, but do record the highlights.

Skills – skills are abilities you have had the opportunity to develop through your work, activities, and classes; public speaking, computer knowledge, writing skills, and customer service are all examples of aptitudes to list in this category; the following skills checklist can help you compile your skill set; highlight any you believe apply to your experiences.

    ____ Public Speaking Skills

    ____ Computer Knowledge

    ____ Writing Skills

    ____ Goal Oriented

    ____ Creative

    ____ Ability to function as part of a team

    ____ Decision Making Ability

    ____ Leadership Skills

    ____ Problem Solving Abilities

_____ Research Skills

_____ Analyzing Skills

_____ Ability to see more than one
solution to a problem

_____ Organizational Skills

_____ Attention to Detail

_____ Initiative

EXAMPLE OF A RESUME'

Harrison J. Jordan

1234 Success Hall, Rock Hill, SC

803-123-4567

harrisonjordan@success.com

Education

University of Success (expected graduation
May, 2020)

- Enrolled in the School of Success and
Drive

Diploma, Success High School (May, 2016)

- Graduated with 3.56/4.0 GPA

- Enrolled in Honors and Advanced Placement Courses

Coursework

Current courses fulfill School's General Success Requirements

- Highlights include: Believe 101, Introduction to Failure & Success

Employment

Student Employee, Career Development Office, University of Success

- Assist with administrative duties as assigned

Camp Counselor, SMJ Parks and Recreation (Summer 2008)

- Organized and supervised activities for Youth Day Camp

- Provided safe and fun environment for kids ages 6-11

Activities

Writer, Success High School Yearbook (2007-2008)

Member, Success High School Chorus (2005-2008)

Member, Success High School Tennis Team (2005-2008)

Volunteer Work

Community Service Participant, St. Luke Baptist Church

- Participated in various Outreach Programs through Church involvement

FINANCIAL AID TIPS

1. Don't participate in a shopping spree.

2. Don't buy rims or jewelry.

3. Don't spend the money before the next Semester.

4. Don't dine out.

5. Don't use your check on non-school items if possible.

6. Don't sign a rental agreement.

7. Don't buy a new car (remember car payments last longer than the refund check amount).

8. Don't tell everyone you have a refund check.

9. Send extra money back to student loan provider.

10. Invest the money in an interest bearing Savings Account.

11. Pay any balances on high interest rate credit cards (student loan interest rates are between 1% and 3%).

12. Be responsible with your refund check, it is not a paycheck.

GOING TO COLLEGE:
Quick Resource Guide for You It's never too late or too early to start applying!

HIGH SCHOOL

COLLEGE

MIDDLE SCHOOL

Grants

Parents

Freshman

Take Action

FASFA.ED.GOV – APPLY

TODAY!!!

Q. What is FAFSA?

A. *Free Application for Federal Student Aid*

Q. What is federal financial aid?

A. *Federal student aid covers such expenses as tuition and fees, room and board, books and supplies, and transportation. Aid also can help pay for a computer and for dependent care.*

Q. What is the eligibility for FAFSA?

A. *Be a U.S. citizen, a U.S. national or eligible noncitizen .*

Be registered with Selective Service if you are male.

Be attending a participating school.

Be working toward a degree or certifi-cate in an eligible program.

Be making satisfactory academic pro-gress.

Q. What kind of federal financial aid is available?

A. There are four categories of federal financial aid:

Grant—Grant money usually doesn't have to be repaid. Most U.S. Depart-ment of Education grants are based on the student's financial need.

- **Scholarship**—U.S. Department of Education scholarship money is awarded based on a student's academic achievement and does not have to be repaid.

■ *Work-study*—Work-study money is earned by a student through a job on or near campus while attending school and does not have to be re-paid.

■ *Loan*—Loan money must be repaid with interest. For details about the federal student aid programs, includ-ing maximum annual amounts and loan interest rates, visit www.Federal-StudentAid.ed.gov/guide.

Q. Why would I apply for a federal loan?

A. Federal student loans offer low fixed interest rates; income-based repayment plans; loan forgiveness; and deferment options, including deferment of loan *payments when a student returns to school. Generally, repayment of a federal loan does not begin until after the student leaves school. Did you know that a student receiving a federal loan does not need acredit history or a cosigner? Private loans from banks often do not offer such benefits. So if you need to borrow money to pay for college or trade school, start with federal student loans.*

FYI

There is no "secret" scholarship money out there. You don't need to pay a consultant or join a society just because they say they can help you find scholarships.

You can find them yourself and save some money!

Where do I apply for FAFSA?

You must complete and submit a Free Application for Federal Student Aid (FAFSA^{SM}) to apply for federal student aid and most state and college aid. FAFSA on the Web^{SM} is the quickest and easiest method of applying. http://www.fafsa.ed.gov

★ ★ ★ ★ ★ ★ ★ ★

SCHOLARSHIP INFO:

☞ Visit <u>www.students.gov</u> to find out about education funding available from other federal agencies.

☞ Visit <u>www.ed.gov/Programs/ bastmp/SHEA.htm</u> to find out about money available from state governments.

☞ Visit a college's Web site or ask its financial aid office about money the school offers its students

MORE SCHOLARSHIP IDEAS

☞ the U.S. Department of Education's FREE online scholarship

☞ search at www.FederalStudentAid.ed.gov/scholarship

☞ a high school, Upward Bound, or Talent Search counselor

☞ your library's reference section

☞ foundations, religious or community organizations,

☞ local businesses, or civic groups

☞ organizations (including professional associations)

☞ related to your field of interest

☞ ethnicity-based organizations

☞ your employer or your parents' (parent's)

☞ employers (employer)

11 FORTUNE BUILDING STEPS FOR STUDENTS

1.   **Fear is Not an Option**
     a.   Acknowledge your fear
     b.   Release Fear
     c.   Change Thoughts

2.   **Envision Your Destiny**
     a.   Know that your past is not your future
     b.   Where do you see yourself in the future?
     c.   What are you going to do to create the results you desire?

3.   **Take Action**
     a.   Map Out Plan
     b.   Set Goals
     c.   Do Something Now

4. **Set Yourself Apart**

    a.   Evaluate your Strengths & Weaknesses

    b.   Create a Resume' & Cover Letter

    c.   Develop Communication Skills

5. **Networking=Net worth**

    a.   Business Cards

    b.   Learn how to Build Effective Relationships

    c.   Examples of Relationships: mutually beneficial, investing, receiving, etc.

6. **Be Persistent & Committed**

    a.   Overcome rejections

    b.   For Every 10 No's there is a Yes

    c.   Hard Work Pays Off

7.   **Determine Your Value**

   a.   What are you worth?

   b.   Do Your Research

   c.   Don't Settle for less

8.   **Create Your Own Opportunities**

   Resource Opportunities

   a.   Internet

   b.   Career Centers

   c.   Financial Aid Office

   d.   Organizations/ Professional Associations

9.   **Follow-Up & Follow-thru**

   a.   How many missed opportunities from lack of following-thru?

   b.   Thank you Letter, calls, e-mails

10. Adopt Leadership Qualities

    a.   Learn something new everyday

    b.   Evaluate options

    c.   Articulate goals

    d.   Determine plan

    e.   Empower yourself

    f.   Recognize opportunities

    g.   Strategize success

11. Never Give Up

COLLEGE VISIT SUMMARY SHEET

Before visiting a college be sure to review carefully the information in the school brochure or Web site. Upon completion of your visit, write your responses to the following issues. Do this for each college visited and then compare your summaries for each.

College or University: _____

Location: _____

Date of Visit: _____

Interviewer: _____

Student Body

(Impression of student body in terms of appearance, style, friendliness, degree of interest and enthusiasm, diversity of social, religious, and ethnic background.)

_____

_____

_____

Academic Factors

(How serious about academics is the college and its students; how good are the facilities for academic pursuits; how varied is the curriculum; how strict or flexible are the requirements; how appropriate is the college for your interests?)

_____

_____

_____

Campus Facilities and Social Life

(How complete and modern are the facilities, such as dorms, library, Internet system, student center, athletic complex; how active is the social life; how diverse is it; is it a suitcase or commuter campus?)

_____

_____

_____

Overall Impressions

(What did you like least and most; what seemed different or special. What type of student do you feel would be happiest there? Are you the type?)

_____

_____

_____

_____

Rating

(On a scale of 1 to 5, with 1 being the top grade, rate the college on the basis of your interest in it.)

_____

_____

_____

_____

****Keep a journal of your experience****

FINANCIAL AID WORKSHEET

Expense	Due Date	Present Amount	Projected Future Amount
One-Year Budget			
Colleges			
Tuition			
Room and board Fees			
Books and supplies			
Travel			
Personal expenses			
Total			
Kinds of Financial Aid Available			
Tuition payment plans			
Monthly payments			
Four years payable in advance			

Scholarships			
Student loans from the college			
Government aid plans administered by the college			
Campus jobs available			
Hours per week			
Non-campus jobs available			
Summer job leads			
Financial counseling			
Due Dates			
Miscellaneous Expenses			

AFFIRMATIONS FOR THE STUDENT'S SOUL

- I am a successful student.

- I am able to make friends easily.

- I will achieve high grades.

- I am happy.

- I feel good about myself.

- I love and respect myself.

- I know I am important.

- I am somebody, and I count.

- I do well in school.

- I love smiling and giving others compliments.

- I am motivated by both successes and failures.

- I think before I speak.

- I learn from my mistakes.

- I strive to improve myself.

- Every day I am getting better and better.

- I have positive self-esteem.

- I accept myself completely as I am.

- I take charge of my life.

- I am valuable.

- I am confident.

- I am success.

www.ingramcontent.com/pod-product-compliance
Lightning Source LLC
LaVergne TN
LVHW021524080426
835509LV00018B/2655